EXPLORING
CAREERS

Careers in Digital Media

ReferencePoint
Press®

Other titles in the *Exploring Careers* series include:

Careers in Business Administration
Careers in Computer Science
Careers in Entertainment
Careers in Environmental Conservation
Careers in Medicine

EXPLORING
CAREERS

Careers in Digital Media

Laura Roberts

ReferencePoint
Press®

© 2018 ReferencePoint Press, Inc.
Printed in the United States

For more information, contact:
ReferencePoint Press, Inc.
PO Box 27779
San Diego, CA 92198
www.ReferencePointPress.com

LIBRARY OF CONGRESS CATALOGING-IN-PUBLICATION DATA

Name: Roberts, Laura, 1978– author.
Title: Careers in Digital Media/by Laura Roberts.
Description: San Diego, CA: ReferencePoint Press, Inc., 2017. | Series: Exploring Careers | Includes bibliographical references and index.
Identifiers: LCCN 2016056809 (print) | LCCN 2017024050 (ebook) | ISBN 9781682821978 (eBook) | ISBN 9781682821961 (hardback)
Subjects: LCSH: Online journalism—Vocational guidance—Juvenile literature. | Digital media—Vocational guidance—Juvenile literature.
Classification: LCC PN4784.O62 (ebook) | LCC PN4784.O62 R625 2017 (print) | DDC 302.23/1023--dc23
LC record available at https://lccn.loc.gov/2016056809

Contents

An Exploding Field

The digital media industry is growing by leaps and bounds. More and more Americans are packing vast computing power into portable electronics like powerful cell phones and tablets, and jobs are increasingly becoming mobile. As high-speed Internet access becomes more accessible and affordable for the average person, more jobs are going fully digital. It has become commonplace for employees to work from home, from coffee shops, or even in coworking spaces designed to mimic the communal feeling of a traditional office. Reporting on its Implications of Digital Media Survey, the World Economic Forum in 2016 stated that "almost 70% of participants agree that the use of digital media for work-related purposes has already grown significantly and that it will continue to do so in the future."

Internet access, in particular, is expanding. According to a March 2015 White House blog post, 98 percent of Americans are connected to high-speed wireless networks. Additionally, according to the National Broadband Map, US urban and rural populations are almost evenly matched when it comes to high-speed Internet access. With so much Internet accessibility for all citizens, growth of digital jobs is likely to follow.

What Is Digital Media?

Digital media refers to a variety of methods of communication available online. Although digital media includes traditional media outlets such as newspapers, magazines, books, film, radio, and television, it also includes an even wider variety of communications, such as blogs and websites, e-books, streaming videos, photos and artistic images, social media, and much more. Careers in digital media, therefore, cover a vast spectrum and can include everything from content creation to jobs that help people buy, sell, organize, sift, and sort through the barrage of media increasingly found online. From creators of digital or tangible content selling their wares through online marketplaces such as Amazon and Etsy, to individuals selling goods and services on their own websites, there are hundreds—even thousands—of new jobs popping up every day.

And as more and more people turn to the Internet for shopping, gaming, job hunting, and conducting all types of business, the marketplace becomes ever more digital. Jobs like digital content specialist, global campaigns project manager, web designer, and digital media strategist are gaining popularity. And even as print media is declining, online journalists continue to report the news and bring new life to the field. Individuals from publicists to musicians are using the Internet to access new job opportunities, and there are more and more career choices that make use of these new and evolving technologies.

Forever Following Flexibility

Flexibility is one of the key factors in the growth of digital media careers. Today's employees demand more free time, as well as more work hours, and want the flexibility to complete their tasks according to their own schedules. Instead of working directly for a boss, who may dictate certain projects and leave too much or too little wiggle room in schedules, digital workers typically set their own hours and create schedules that work best for them. So long as the work gets done by a set deadline, all is well. As Simon Slade, chief executive officer of the affiliate marketing training website Affilorama, explains in a CMSWire article, "Nothing telegraphs how much you trust your employees [more] than the freedom to set their own hours. And that's exactly what I do in my own company." Digital media careers are also great for employees with families, as such careers allow them a chance to work around family members with more rigid schedules (such as taking kids to school or extracurricular activities) and spread out their work hours over different parts of the day. In addition to scheduling flexibility, digital workers also frequently want to be able to travel.

Careers in Digital Arts

Occupation	Related Titles	2016 Median Salary
Creative director	Art director, design director, creative services director	$102,000
Digital copywriter	Content strategist, content creator, copy editor, technical copywriter	$63,000
Digital designer	Visual designer, Web designer, integrated designer, interactive designer	$72,000
Digital marketing manager	Digital media manager, online marketing manager, Web marketing manager, marketing manager	$87,000
Digital producer	Interactive producer, Web production manager, multimedia producer, video producer, product manager	$71,000
Email marketing manager	Email marketing analyst, push marketing specialist, campaign marketer	$66,000
Front-end Web developer	UI developer, Web developer, HTML5 developer, WordPress developer, interactive developer, Flash developer	$85,000
Full stack Web developer	UX developer, Android developer, IOS developer, mobile developer, product developer, application developer	$106,000
Graphic designer	Packaging designer, presentation designer, 2D designer, graphic editor, illustrator, graphic artist, multimedia designer, experimental designer	$55,000
Interactive project manager	Digital project manager, creative services project manager, traditional project manager, project lead, program lead, program manager	$83,000
Marketing analyst	Marketing operations analyst, campaign analyst	$60,000
Presentation designer	PowerPoint designer, keynote designer, infographic designer, CAD designer	$60,000
Product designer	UI designer, interaction designer, visual designer, interface designer	$96,000
SEM manager	Search engine marketing manager, SEO manager, paid search manager, SEM analyst, implementation specialist	$91,000
Social media manager	Community manager, brand ambassador, search marketing manager	$62,000
UX designer	UX product designer, UI designer, usability researcher, mobile UX designer, information architect	$100,000

ource: Bureau of Labor Statistics, C

By escaping from the office cubicle, they can work anywhere they please—including on the beach or from a foreign country they have always wanted to explore. Indeed, this kind of mobility is exactly what draws many people to digital media careers.

Major Areas of Study

The digital media industry is a great choice for students interested in a wide variety of academic fields. Combining elements of fine art, computer technology and design, writing, and editing, digital media incorporates multimedia disciplines from across a wide spectrum. Creativity and technological skills are both necessary to work in this industry, and some of the most successful employees often end up collaborating on projects or relying on a strong network of fellow freelancers in order to complete a variety of tasks. Writers may find work as freelance writers, web journalists, or social media managers. Fine artists and visual artists may become involved with graphic design, web design, web development, or even film and video editing. Those with leadership skills may become digital project managers, digital marketing strategists, or even digital media specialists.

Ultimately, digital media is becoming the way people do business, and more and more jobs are being added to the digital sphere each day. As the online world expands, so do career opportunities for those who seek them.

Freelance Writer

What Does a Freelance Writer Do?

Freelance writers who work in digital media create content for a variety of websites. These writers may focus on writing for entertainment, informational, or educational purposes, or even to help market online goods and services. They may be responsible for writing blogs, articles, lists (or listicles), and more. Some work as regular contributors to websites; others write pieces for a patchwork of sites that need content. Many different types of freelance writing careers can be found in the digital world. Among them are copywriters, who perfect content for sales pages, e-mail marketing, home pages, and reports; content writers; bloggers; ghostwriters, who produce material published under someone else's name; and journalists.

While some freelance writers write many different types of things for lots of different audiences, many try to offer expertise in one specific niche, or area of interest. Trying to choose which area to focus on can be difficult for those who are just starting out. It takes time to build a reputation and a good relationship with website editors, but those writers who

At a Glance

Freelance Writer

Minimum Educational Requirements
Flexible

Personal Qualities
Creativity and storytelling skills, strong written communication skills, self-directed, technical skills

Working Conditions
Home or office

Salary Range
About $60,250 to $65,000

Number of Jobs
As of 2014, about 136,500

Future Job Outlook
Growth rate of 2 percent to 4 percent through 2024

work diligently often have no shortage of assignments. As writer C. Hope Clark notes on the Write Life website, the best way to figure out where to begin as a freelance writer is to determine any long-term goals, as well as how much money will be necessary to achieve those goals, and what the writer is willing to write about in order to earn that money. Clark advises writers to "list three assets that define you," as well as "three things that inspire you" and "three things you dream about," to help writers define their areas of expertise and create a list of topics to write about. She sums all of this up as "organization and drive": the two key factors in becoming a successful freelance writer.

Freelance writers are always adding to their portfolio, their body of work that they can present to a prospective editor or website manager. The more impressive their portfolio, the more these writers will be able to choose which assignments to take. Usually, more experienced writers can demand higher pay for their work. Demonstrating an ability to write well, meet deadlines, and keep the trust of their employers is how freelance writers build engaging and profitable careers.

How Do You Become a Freelance Writer?

Education

There is no degree in freelance writing, but one logical course of study for a would-be freelance writer is a liberal arts degree. Students in such fields of study typically learn how to read texts carefully, write academic papers on literary subjects, and defend arguments with well-detailed analysis of multiple sources. Most liberal arts programs expose students to a wide range of general subjects, including philosophy, math, literature, art history, economics, and foreign languages, which will expand the number of topics on which they can ultimately write.

While familiarity with a topic or audience and passion for the subject frequently counts more than writing ability, freelance writers do still need excellent writing skills and should work hard to hone their craft. Creative writing degrees can be helpful, depending on what type of writing the freelancer aims to do, and learning the rules and craft of storytelling can also come in handy. In addition to an

Content created by freelance writers working in digital media might be used for entertainment, information, education, or marketing. Platforms also vary; their work might appear in the form of a blog, an article, a listicle, or some other format or combination of these.

undergraduate degree, many schools also offer a master of fine arts in creative writing at the graduate level, which helps writers further develop their skills.

Getting Experience

In addition to academic training, joining a school newspaper, literary magazine, or other campus media outlet will help students hone their writing skills for publication and teach the importance of meeting deadlines. Student writers are often paired with faculty advisors, who can teach additional writing tricks of the trade and help students improve their work outside of the classroom setting. This kind of mentorship is indispensable for students looking to make writing their profession, as faculty members may also be able to recommend work opportunities or write glowing recommendation letters for the students with whom they have worked.

Skills and Personality

Freelance writers need to be able to write well, but they must have other skills, too. Kate Hamill points out on the Freelancers Union blog that writers must also be decent editors of their own work, should be "relatively speedy," and should actually enjoy writing. Not every assignment will be fascinating—especially for those who are just beginning their careers—but freelancers must be able to stick with projects to the end. Otherwise, they may find that editors will not trust them to handle future assignments. Beyond that, freelance writers also need to have a healthy sense of curiosity as well as the ability to turn what they learn into an interesting, readable piece. As freelance writer and business owner Carol Tice suggests in an article on the Make a Living Writing website, "When you're told a piece of news, do you find yourself asking questions about it? Wondering what will happen next? Why this thing has happened? And then, do you feel compelled to learn more? This is an essential for any writer. You need to explore. To ask questions. To know. And to share what you find out with the world through the written word."

Freelance writers must also have a knack for solving problems—especially for their clients. Freelance writer Frankie Thompson explains in a Fizzle article, "You are not a writer. You are a problem solver. People looking for freelancers are looking for that person to perform a service or create a product that solves a problem they can't fix on their own." Whether that means copywriting, creating original content, or anything else a client requests, Thompson is right to note that freelance writers must be strong problem solvers. After all, they never quite know what might get dropped into their laps—and being able to view challenges as opportunities can endear a tenacious freelancer to a client.

In addition to problem solving, freelance writers must absolutely be self-directed, self-motivated people. With no boss setting a daily schedule, freelancers of all kinds need to understand how to set their own goals, block out the appropriate amount of time to reach them, and stay on task. Students who find independent study a positive thing will most likely gravitate toward the solitude that the freelance life affords. In addition to being left on one's own, freelancers must be self-motivated, with plenty of persistence to keep them going through the rough times. As freelance writer Laura Kay explains in an article in the *Guardian*, "Whichever way you get into freelancing, the absolute key to success is persistence. Chances are you'll get knocked back a fair bit but keeping going is the only way to ensure that you get noticed."

Finally, freelance writers must have excellent technical and online skills, as most of their work will be done online. The ability to do quick online research, locate sources for interviews, and deal with all kinds of software programs is key to a freelance writer's success. Being able to learn new software and skills on the fly and quickly apply new information to whatever situation comes up is an indispensable skill.

On the Job

Employers

Freelance writers typically work for a wide variety of companies. Depending on their subject matter and niche, some may write for well-known general interest magazines, like *Reader's Digest* or *Time*. Others may work for entertainment magazines and websites, like *People* magazine or TMZ. Still others may perform ghostwriting duties for major companies, writing blog posts or articles that members of the company will be credited with writing. For every subject imaginable, there is a corresponding list of magazines, websites, and corporations where writers are needed to churn out online articles, essays, and even fictional works.

Since freelance writers are, by definition, working for many different employers at once, they are considered contract workers and are typically paid per story or per word, rather than with hourly wages or salary. The more streams, or outlets, a writer works for, the more income he or she typically earns. As freelance writer Tim Leffel notes in an article on the Make a Living Writing website, "I surveyed 82 people when putting together the second edition of my book *Travel Writing 2.0*. The travel writers who are making $100,000 or more annually have one key thing in common. They all have 10 or more income streams related to travel." So rather than focusing on just one or two media outlets, the best thing for freelance writers to do is diversify their writing portfolio and continue to land new clients.

Working Conditions

Freelance writers typically work from home, although travel to and from an office may occasionally be required. More and more, however, freelance writers have flexible working schedules, with meetings scheduled virtually via Skype or similar video-chatting applications. As the Bureau of Labor Statistics (BLS) notes, freelance writers typically work full time or part time in a home office, with varied schedules.

Earnings

Although the BLS does not make a distinction between work in digital and traditional media, the bureau reports that full-time freelance writers can expect to earn around $60,250 per year, depending on their skills and expertise. According to information obtained from the job-search website Indeed in October 2016, typical freelance writers make an average of $65,000 a year. As freelance writer Linda Formichelli explains in a Fizzle article, "Writing at a breakneck pace is my number one secret when it comes to earning more. The faster you write, the more you earn."

Opportunities for Advancement

Freelance writing for digital media is open to newcomers but also rewards those who spend time developing additional skills and expertise. The more specialized a subject, the more a freelancer can expect to be paid for his or her expertise. Conversely, of course, the more broad a topic, the more competition there will be for those writing about those subjects, and therefore pay rates will be much less competitive. The best ways for freelance writers to advance in the field are to continue to learn more about their chosen subject matter, hone their writing skills, and keep up with new technology.

What Is the Future Outlook for Freelance Writers?

The BLS projects a growth rate of 2 percent to 4 percent through 2024 for freelance writers. For those who want to pursue a career as a freelance writer in digital media, hard work is the key to a strong future. As Kate Hamill notes in a Freelancers Union blog post, writers typically do not require writing degrees, and instead must prove themselves through their portfolio of written work. Keeping this in mind, the more freelance work a writer completes, the better his or her job prospects become. Hamill offers this advice: "Seek out help, build a portfolio, find clients, carve out a specialty, and don't expect to succeed overnight."

Find Out More

Make a Living Writing
www.makealivingwriting.com

This website offers practical advice for aspiring freelance writers, as well as existing freelancers looking for more information on how to build their skills and portfolios or improve their pay rates.

Media Bistro
825 Eighth Avenue
New York, NY 10019
www.mediabistro.com

A great career site for anyone searching for jobs in media, including freelance writers. Check the job list, read how-to articles and interviews with career insiders, and take classes to sharpen your skills.

Men with Pens
www.menwithpens.ca

Despite its name, this website is actually run by a woman and aims to keep freelance writers educated and informed on everything related to the art and craft of copywriting.

The Write Life
www.thewritelife.com

A website dedicated to helping writers create, connect, and earn, this is an excellent resource for finding paying markets, job listings, and information about how to become a full-time writer.

Writer's Digest
www.writersdigest.com

This magazine and website aims to help writers achieve their goals. In addition to tons of great practical advice for writers in all genres, *Writer's Digest* also publishes an annual list of the 101 Best Websites for Writers, which highlights advice from across the web.

WritersMarket.com
www.writersmarket.com

A great place to find paying markets for any type of freelance writing, including short fiction, poetry, personal essays, and more.

Social Media Manager

What Does a Social Media Manager Do?

Social media managers are digital public relations specialists. They represent a brand or company online and are typically considered the public face of those companies. They respond to comments and criticism on behalf of the company, as well as engage members of the online community and encourage people to follow the company's various social media profiles. This is done with a mix of content creation and customer service skills and is aimed at creating friendly interaction between individuals and a brand.

In addition to creating a variety of content, social media managers are also responsible for coming up with strategies for digital marketing campaigns, as well as analyzing their results. Social media managers track digital traffic driven to a company's website through different social media sites and analyze the content that results in the most conversions (or sales) to make sure the company can continue to use strategies that work

---

At a Glance

Social Media Manager

Minimum Educational Requirements
Flexible

Personal Qualities
Strong written communication skills, time-management skills, customer service skills, visual thinking

Working Conditions
Home or office

Salary Range
About $47,000 to $61,000

Number of Jobs
As of 2014, about 240,700

Future Job Outlook
Growth rate of 6 percent through 2024

---

and avoid those that do not. Social media managers also use this information, known as analytics, to continue to build a website's audience.

In short, a social media manager is both a skilled social media user and a marketing and advertising expert, all rolled into one. As a 2016 article by social media strategist Kathi Kruse on Kruse Control Inc. put it:

> The Social Media Manager will administer the company's social media marketing and advertising. Administration includes but is not limited to: deliberate planning and goal setting, development of brand awareness and online reputation, content management, SEO (search engine optimization) and generation of inbound traffic, [and] cultivation of leads and sales.

Social media managers like Suzanne Samin, who works for Romper (a millennial-focused parenting site) are also responsible for selecting and presenting relevant information for the website's social media accounts. It is Samin's job, according to an interview that appears on Mediabistro, to "monitor, moderate and respond to audience comments; manage social media partnerships with other brands; and create and/or post shareable videos and images."

How Do You Become a Social Media Manager?

Education

Although there are no specific educational prerequisites for becoming a social media manager, there are a few fields of study that lend themselves to learning about social media. One good field of study is the Digital Studies certificate program, available at the University of Wisconsin–Madison. The program explores relationships between communications and digital technology and offers a multidisciplinary approach with courses in art, communication arts, journalism, life science communication, English, and library and information studies. According to the school's website, "The Digital Studies curriculum provides students the opportunity to both produce digital content and critically assess the digital content they encounter." The University of Pittsburgh–Greensburg also offers a Digital Studies certificate, and Johns Hopkins University offers a Digital Curation certificate program. Many schools are developing similar programs to help students learn how to master digital media.

Another good field of study is communications, which includes digital media and helps students learn more about communications careers of all kinds. Most liberal arts colleges and universities have a communications major available for undergraduates, as well as more-advanced degrees for those with a strong interest in this area.

Getting Experience

Individuals who want to work as social media managers typically start out by building their own social media communities. As writer Scott Ayres points out in an article on Post Planner,

> Before you can sign up clients you'll probably need to have a thriving social media presence of your own. Create accounts on all the major social media websites and familiarize yourself with blogging, email marketing, search engine optimization and graphic design. If you can't market yourself . . . you'll never be able to market for others!

Social media managers typically learn the career skills they need by doing this kind of work on their own. Ultimately, this is a lot like learning on the job, but in this case, the "job" is promoting oneself instead of a company. Ayres also recommends experimenting with advanced marketing techniques such as "optimizing YouTube videos with descriptions, tags, titles, annotations, etc.; [creating] custom Facebook apps; [creating] custom Twitter and YouTube headers; knowledge of hashtag marketing; knowledge of webcasts, Google+ Hangouts, email capture forms, etc."

Skills and Personality

Social media managers require a variety of different skills, as their job covers many different tasks. The first and most important skill is copywriting ability. Not only are communication skills an important part of the job, but being able to effectively sell a company's products or services to consumers is at the core of everything a social media manager does. In a Mediabistro blog post, writer Jenell Talley notes, "Top-notch communication and writing skills are important . . . as is a good sense of humor. . . . Just remember to keep your brand and audience in mind when crafting your message."

In addition to writing skills and a sense of humor, social media managers also need to be on top of time management. Juggling a variety of different projects and social media accounts means that social media managers are often running in a dozen directions at once. Time management skills are therefore critical to being able to stay on task, meet goals, and get through all of the day's work.

Along with being able to manage time wisely, social media managers must also have what *Forbes* writer Jayson DeMers calls a "customer-service mindset." Describing the skills he believes a social media manager must master, DeMers notes, "Posting pithy or clever sayings, captivating images and inspirational content will only get you so far if you're not responding appropriately to customer-service queries." Indeed, he suggests that social media managers should respond quickly to both questions and complaints, in order to prove that the company is customer focused. He also points out that since social media managers are considered the face of the brand online, they therefore need to represent that brand in a positive light at all times.

In addition to customer service skills, social media managers must be very tech savvy. They must be well versed in how to use all social media sites, including Facebook, Twitter, Instagram, Pinterest, Snapchat, and many more. They must also be familiar with scheduling apps (such as Hootsuite, Buffer, and others) in order to quickly and efficiently complete their tasks and to preschedule posts days, weeks, or even months in advance. Along with using these social media platforms, social media managers are required to become experts in all kinds of content creation and editing apps, including services that focus on text, still images, videos, and podcasts. As the digital media field continues to grow, being able to keep up with increasing technological advances and a wide variety of apps and services will be key to a social media manager's success.

On the Job

Employers

A wide variety of companies employ social media managers; most such positions are full-time and draw a salary. The kinds of companies they work for can range from multimillion-dollar internationally recognized ones, like the Coca-Cola Company and the Nokia Corporation, to smaller mom-and-pop shops looking for someone to manage their online presence. Since virtually every company has a need for social media management, whether they know it or not, enterprising freelancers can also build a name for themselves by seeking out local or small businesses to represent online.

Working Conditions

Managing social media accounts for a big corporation can be tricky. An ability to juggle a variety of information streams and media concerns is key to any social media manager's success. Amy Guth, the social media manager for the Tribune Media Group, notes in a GotInterviews piece that she and her social media partner "try hard to balance the breaking news that requires swift action, with the steps in our other projects that aren't so time-sensitive, meetings, training sessions and that sort of thing."

This brings up an important point: Social media managers rarely work alone. Indeed, Kevan Lee, director of marketing for social sharing app Buffer, says that he has found the job to be a team effort, with one person working on updates, one working on engagement, and a whole team of people working on "support, response, and happiness." Since Lee is the manager of the group, he predominantly fills Buffer's social media streams with blog content, announcements, and inspirational posts. Meanwhile, one of his coworkers writes posts that "engage the community with questions." This coworker also hosts a weekly Twitter chat and replies to comments every day, along with a total of ten Buffer employees who also help with social media management throughout the week.

Being able to remain calm while being pulled in so many different directions by customer comments or complaints is crucial to a social media manager's success. Having a large number of tasks to deal with on any given day means that most social media managers work long hours and can be on call throughout late nights and early mornings.

Earnings

According to the job site PayScale, social media managers can expect to earn around $47,000 per year, depending on their skills and expertise. According to information obtained on the job-search website Indeed in November 2016, typical social media managers make an average of $61,000 a year.

Opportunities for Advancement

The more a social media manager builds up his or her portfolio, the more opportunities there are for advancement. Naturally, those who work with bigger clients can earn more money, but there is also a level of expertise and experience required in order to reach those upper levels. Social media managers may also work with teams, creating strategies with brand managers or an entire advertising firm, which means they may occasionally find themselves moving up the ladder as new players enter and leave their companies.

What Is the Future Outlook for Social Media Managers?

The Bureau of Labor Statistics projects a growth rate of 6 percent through 2024 for public relations specialists like social media managers. Although in many companies today all employees need to be savvy with social media, social media managers still have a special role to play. While many different employees are being tasked with social media manager duties regarding the online content they produce for a company, most employees are not entirely prepared for the task. Indeed, social media managers have specific expertise in this area, because it is their sole focus. As companies continue to refine their social media strategies and hire new recruits to help implement them, the role of the social media manager will continue to gain importance. Leaders in this field will stand out by helping others learn from their experiences and by helping train them in the do's and don'ts of social media engagement.

Find Out More

Kissmetrics Blog
http://blog.kissmetrics.com

Billed as a blog about analytics, marketing, and testing, the Kissmetrics company blog covers all kinds of social media tools and tricks for keeping current in this ever-changing field. Kissmetrics also offers software that can help users understand their own website's analytics.

Razor Social
www.razorsocial.com

A great resource for aspiring social media managers looking for tips and tricks on how to wrangle the top social media websites. The site also offers a free "cheat sheet" for inexpensive or free social media tools to those who sign up for the site's mailing list.

Social Media Examiner
www.socialmediaexaminer.com

A guide to social media, this site includes a blog, a podcast, and links to in-person events like the annual Social Media Marketing World expo in San Diego. A great resource for learning more about social media, as new developments are chronicled daily.

Social Media Today
www.socialmediatoday.com

An online community and resource for professionals in marketing, social business, communication, customer experience, content marketing, and digital strategy, making it a great resource for anyone who aspires to get into these businesses as well.

Unmetric
http://blog.unmetric.com

The blog for Unmetric is a great place to learn how to outperform your competition. With articles and advice on social analytics, industry reports, and analysis, this company blog is a great way to learn about all of social media's latest and greatest hits, hacks, and fails.

Web Journalist

What Does a Web Journalist Do?

Web journalists (known these days simply as journalists) report the news online, using audiovisual storytelling techniques. They are typically responsible for creating both print and video (or sometimes audio-only) presentations of the same story, and making both available to an online audience. As the Learn How to Become website notes, "At the most basic level, journalists investigate, collect, and present information. Journalists do this in newspapers and magazines, but it can also be done in radio and television broadcasts, and online, through websites, blogs, podcasts, and other digital platforms." Indeed, the craft of journalism has changed so much in the past few years that it now has a larger presence in the digital realm than in the more traditional print and broadcast world. As the same website points out, journalism is all about investigation and reporting on subjects or issues that are of importance to the public. This means that journalists must use their skills—along with a variety of technical tools—to properly package a story in order to gain and hold readers' attention. Online journalists must be skilled

At a Glance

Web Journalist

Minimum Educational Requirements
Bachelor's degree

Personal Qualities
Critical-thinking skills, strong written communication skills, relationship-building skills

Working Conditions
Home or office

Salary Range
About $36,360 to $105,620

Number of Jobs
As of 2014, about 54,400

Future Job Outlook
Slow growth through 2024

in various formats, including the creation of videos and podcasts. The more skills one has in different formats, the wider the potential audience. Web journalists must also be comfortable with interviewing people on a range of topics. Some journalists interview subjects in person, while others rely more heavily on phone or videoconferencing interviews, or even e-mailing sources for opinions.

How Do You Become a Web Journalist?

Education

To become a web journalist, the best field of study is journalism. Journalism schools teach students how to cultivate (and protect) story sources, maintain objectivity and balance both sides of a story, be skeptical, investigate stories, and report all the facts in the best order to create a compelling and well-written story. As Northwestern University's Medill School of Journalism explains its program, professors "teach undergraduates how to be communicators who can adapt to the changing media landscape." Offering a variety of residencies and internships, the school promotes mobile journalism based in Washington, DC, and California's Bay Area, as well as justice-focused reporting that examines areas like wrongful convictions and systemic criminal justice issues. Students, therefore, receive both classroom training and on-the-job immersion in what journalists do every day, combining practical and theoretical knowledge.

Those who plan to specialize in a specific subject area such as business, environment, or technology, for instance, should consider course work in those subjects. For example, budding business writers may want to study business, economics, or statistics in order to more fully understand the topic on which they are reporting. Would-be science reporters should study chemistry, biology, physics, or similar fields in order to offer readers keen insights into the technical information that appears in their stories. In short, being able to explain technical terminology and jargon is extremely useful for reporters in specialized areas and will help bring their writing out of niche publications and into the forefront of mainstream media.

Like any other journalists, web journalists gather and report news. Critical thinking, accuracy, ability to interview subjects, and ability to synthesize large amounts of information are important skills for web journalist—as are technical skills for working in digital formats.

Internships

Internships are key for aspiring web journalists. Although online skills are essential for anyone who hopes to work in digital media, learning the basics of journalism is even more important. As *Charlotte (NC) Observer* business reporter Caroline McMillan notes in an interview on The Muse website, references from her journalism school professors were what helped her land her first job, but she also notes that "no amount of good references would have gotten me the job if I didn't have strong clips (from multiple newspapers and publications) and experience (I was Editor-in-Chief of a magazine on campus and a columnist for another)." Since on-the-job experience is what helps journalists improve, being able to intern with a newspaper, magazine, or website is a critical piece of the puzzle when it comes to landing a full-time job in the field. As McMillan observes, even writing for a campus magazine or newspaper counts.

Many media outlets offer summer internships. Some of these are paid positions, while others offer honorariums (small cash sums). The *New York Times*, for example, offers several different paid ten-week summer internships to undergraduate and graduate students majoring in journalism. Internships such as this one are highly competitive. Approaching smaller and possibly even newer media outlets about internship opportunities might prove more fruitful for many aspiring online journalists.

Skills and Personality

One of the most important skills for a web journalist is the ability to think critically. As the Learn How to Become website indicates:

> People who have successful careers in journalism tend to have a few things in common: they are critical thinkers who can access, synthesize, and retain factual information logically and systematically; they are motivated and persistent in their efforts to get at the best available or obtainable version of the truth, and then to verify those facts; they are good communicators who have an intuitive understanding of storytelling and the non-fiction narrative devices that create drama, tension, and suspense.

Being able to think critically is a key component for journalists, not only because their job involves writing stories that present facts in a logical order, but also because the job involves weaving together a story that takes information from many different sources. Picking and choosing appropriate facts, figures, and quotes requires critical thinking as well as good research skills. The best journalists are able to weave together a great deal of information using a limited number of words.

In addition to critical-thinking skills, web journalists also need to be able to build relationships quickly. As web journalist Jenna Goudreau puts it:

> This is a relationship business. If I could turn back time, I would have invested even more in building

and maintaining strong relationships with mentors, colleagues and peers. Journalism professors are often working in the field and can introduce you to the right people. Many of your classmates and internship peers will go on to work in the industry and can make great contacts. Your bosses and colleagues, whether they remain in your company or leave, can advocate for you if a position opens up. Additionally, good relationships with sources and subjects will make you better at your job. Do not underestimate or shortchange your relationships.

Good relationships are vital to obtaining better positions within the industry, and so is the ability to build relationships with sources in order to produce great stories. Having a wealth of sources available on a moment's notice is a journalist's biggest asset.

Web journalists also need to have technical skills. As the website JournalismDegree.com suggests: "Hone your technical skills. Photoshop, HTML, CSS, and web publishing programs are all very important in today's media. Maintain a presence on Facebook, Twitter, Linked-In, and anything else that will get your name out there, help you make connections, and continue to write." In short, mastering any skills that will make reporting work easier is important to a web journalist's success.

On the Job

Employers

A wide variety of newspapers, magazines, blogs, and websites employ web journalists. Reporting opportunities are available everywhere from top-tier news organizations like the *New York Times* to wire services like the Associated Press or Dow Jones. Magazines that publish long-form and independent reporting, such as *Mother Jones* or the *Atlantic*, are also in need of web journalists. Websites and blogs such as Byliner and Epic cover numerous topics and are also frequently in need of web journalists. Web journalists may either be full-time, salaried workers or paid per piece as correspondents, stringers (part-time correspondents), or freelancers.

Working Conditions

Web journalists who are employed by major media companies are often based in big cities. In the United States these would include New York City, Atlanta, Washington, Los Angeles, Dallas, and San Francisco. In other countries it might be London, Hong Kong, Paris, Mexico City, or New Delhi. Web journalism is also a portable job, and talented writers may be able to find work anywhere—especially in places that have more limited media presence.

In addition to choosing a suitable market, another important part of what determines web journalists' working conditions is their level of experience. McMillan describes some of her early jobs in the field, saying that web journalists should give up the idea of a "typical" work-week. In an interview on The Muse website, she explains:

> You might have to pick up a weekend shift. If you're working on a big story, you'll probably have to stay late. And if you're at the bottom of the totem pole—as you will be—the editors might decide you look pretty available when your desk is cleaned up and your computer is shutting down. Then, all you can do is smile, reboot the computer and repeat to yourself: "This is what I love."

Earnings

According to the Bureau of Labor Statistics (BLS), web journalists can expect to earn around $36,360 per year, depending on their skills and expertise. O*NET offers a slightly higher number, suggesting that journalists can make approximately $37,720 per year. At the other end of the spectrum, the job site Glassdoor suggests that *New York Times* journalists make an average of $105,620 a year. According to information obtained on the job-search website Indeed in November 2016, typical journalists make an average of $49,000 a year.

Opportunities for Advancement

Typically, the more a web journalist builds up his or her portfolio, the more opportunities there are for advancement. Entry-level journalists can eventually trade more tedious assignments for better-paid, more interesting assignments the more they build up a body of work. They can also eventually tackle long-form pieces, either solo or as part of a team, giving more in-depth coverage to complex topics. Some journalists will stick with reporting jobs for their entire careers, while others may prefer to transition into editing positions or even managerial jobs.

What Is the Future Outlook for Web Journalists?

Although the BLS suggests that the outlook for web journalists is declining, there are still many jobs available for aspiring journalists who are willing to work hard. Salaried positions may be increasingly difficult to obtain, due to the changing nature of online media, but freelance positions frequently open up at new media outlets. Indeed, journalists are considered the government's "fourth estate"—watchdogs that can help prevent fraud and misconduct by government officials—and therefore they will always be necessary to help the United States maintain a free and democratic society. The field of journalism is undergoing many changes, as citizen journalism continues to expand and fake news sites from around the world proliferate. These challenges can also offer opportunities for trained journalists as the field continues to evolve.

Find Out More

Journalism Jobs
www.journalismjobs.com

A great place to find journalism jobs, featuring a job board, career advice, and the latest media news.

Online Journalism Blog
www.onlinejournalismblog.com

Produced by Paul Bradshaw, head of the MA program in Online Journalism at Birmingham City University, this blog features analysis, commen-
tary, and links about online journalism. Be sure to check out the series of
posts on the 21st Century Newsroom, which offers updated info about how
journalism is evolving in the online era.

Poynter Institute
801 Third St. South
St. Petersburg, FL 33701
www.poynter.org

Founded in 1975, the Poynter Institute has a stated goal of elevating journalism. Offering seminars, online courses, and a variety of news articles,
the institute helps train journalists from around the world and partners
with media organizations like Gannett, Google, National Geographic, and
Univision.

Society of Professional Journalists
Eugene S. Pulliam National Journalism Center
3909 N. Meridian St.
Indianapolis, IN 46208
www.spj.org

With state chapters throughout the United States, this professional society
is dedicated to improving and protecting journalism and has been in exis-
tence since 1909. With nearly seventy-five hundred members, this is a great
professional society to join in order to meet fellow journalists, share their
experience, and protect journalists' right to free speech.

Graphic Designer

Graphic designers create digital art to help present information visually for both online and print media outlets. Graphic designers typically draw from different disciplines, including photography, digital painting and drawing, collage, digital sculpture, and animation. According to the Bureau of Labor Statistics (BLS), "Graphic designers create visual concepts, using computer software or by hand, to communicate ideas that inspire, inform, and captivate consumers. They develop the overall layout and production design for various applications such as advertisements, brochures, magazines, and corporate reports." Graphic design covers a wide area, including marketing materials and digital communication, with branding (creating a name, symbol, or design that helps consumers differentiate between similar products or services) as one of its main goals. As the Art Career Project website puts it, "Most clients hire graphic designers to create something that sends a message. Sometimes this message is loud and clear, but other times it is meant to be subliminal." In short, graphic designers are masters of visual communication.

At a Glance

Graphic Designer

Minimum Educational Requirements

Bachelor's degree

Personal Qualities

Creativity, active-listening skills, critical-thinking skills, team player

Working Conditions

Home or office

Salary Range

About $46,900 to $53,000

Number of Jobs

As of 2014, about 261,600

Future Job Outlook

Growth rate of 1 percent through 2024

Whether working with a design team or going solo, graphic designers convey messages visually using a variety of approaches. They manipulate images (including shapes, colors, and animation) and text to get their message across. As the Learn How to Become website notes:

> Graphic designers must get across a specific message and call-to-action or emotion based on their client's objectives. For instance, a graphic designer may be tasked with creating a brand or logo that makes a lasting impression on consumers, incorporating a unique shape or color scheme.

Because their art is focused on specific types of messaging that may fall into different arenas, graphic designers typically have one or more specialties on which they focus. These can include branding, typography, logo design, web design, book design, product packaging, and user interface or user experience design for websites.

How Do You Become a Graphic Designer?

Education

Graphic designers typically need a bachelor's degree in graphic design or related fields. O*NET indicates that 62 percent of graphic designers hold a bachelor's degree, 15 percent an associate's degree, and 8 percent postsecondary certificates. Students in a graphic design program, such as the program offered by the Rhode Island School of Design, learn how to create and critique the effectiveness of visual communications (including their own and peers' work), respond to potential clients' design needs, develop their own personal methods for creating professional design work, and use both current-day and historical tools of the design trade. Classes typically include traditional drawing and painting courses as well as studio work, and often include additional classes focusing on typography, color theory, spatial dynamics, and explorations into the history of graphic design. Many programs also require students to create a degree project in order to complete their studies and showcase their design skills before graduation. Some graphic designers may also find getting an advanced degree, such as a master of fine arts, to be worthwhile.

Getting Experience

Graphic designers should focus on building their portfolio in order to gain experience. As the BLS notes, "Candidates for graphic design positions should demonstrate their creativity and originality through a professional portfolio that features their best designs." Work done in school can be included in a portfolio. Volunteer work or internships can help an aspiring graphic designer obtain additional work samples. Many big companies offer summer internships for graphic design students. For example, NBCUniversal offers a graphic design/graphic communications internship in Universal City, California. The Walt Disney Company also offers summer graphic design internships, some of which are based in California or New York, while others are available with the company's many global media locations like London, Hong Kong, and Paris. Graphic designer Larry Mayorga also recommends taking on unpaid work for a favorite charity—both to get experience and to make contacts. As he mentions in an article on the *Creative Bloq* blog, "One way to start a network base, add solid work to your portfolio and get noticed is to offer your design skills to charities in your community. . . . Approach a local gallery or business, an animal shelter. Do good work for a really good cause close to your heart."

Skills and Personality

The ideal graphic designer will have both active-listening skills and critical-thinking skills. Since graphic designers spend a great deal of their time creating artwork on behalf of teams of people or companies, they need to be able to listen to the needs of those people and interpret those needs for design purposes. Critical-thinking skills are key to being able to translate what someone who may not be a design expert wants into something that will best represent his or her brand.

Some projects go smoothly, while others may go awry. In both instances, clear communication is essential. In an interview on the *Business of Illustration* blog, graphic designer Kyle T. Webster describes what can happen when communication falls short. "I try to listen very carefully to see if I truly am at fault for having misunderstood the original creative direction," he explains. "If I have truly failed on what I am to have delivered, I make the changes. If I believe that I stuck to the original plan, I try to help the client see how my solution matches up well with their requirements." Ultimately, graphic designers need to be able to actively listen to client requests and defend their own artistic choices when presenting their work.

Graphic designers must also have good people skills. This matters not only for working with clients but also for collaboration with other members of a project team. As Mayorga explains in a *Creative Bloq* post, "We're in a business where making human connections is vital to our growth, regardless of whether we're doing on or off-line work. So being genuinely friendly and interested will hands-down help you to make prospective and repeating clients. Quite simply, building relationships and communication is at the core of our profession, so you can't shy away from it."

Creativity is an essential skill for any graphic designer. Continually coming up with new ideas can be challenging. This may involve coming up with clever ways of saying the same things again and again, or it may involve creating totally new visual representations of things that never previously existed. O*NET Online describes this skill as idea fluency, explaining it as "the ability to come up with a number of ideas about a topic (the number of ideas is important, not their quality, correctness, or creativity)."

On the Job

Employers

Graphic designers who work in digital media may be employed by a wide variety of design firms, publishers, and advertising and public relations groups. Design opportunities are available everywhere, from top design companies like Pentagram, Landor, or MetaDesign to small local businesses in need of a logo. As the Art Career Project website points out, "Graphic designers may also be able to find work with other companies, such as newspapers, magazines, publishers, websites, soft drink companies, museums, and restaurants." Graphic designers may either be full-time, salaried workers or freelancers. The BLS notes that in 2014, approximately one out of five graphic designers were self-employed.

Working Conditions

Graphic designers typically work in studios, whether they are members of a design team headquartered at a large company or solo artists working from home. Studio conditions vary according to the designer, but as illustrator and graphic designer Nicole Martinez explains in an interview with the Arter Designist website, having easy access to coffee and inspirational music are the keys to her success. "I'm Cuban so coffee is essential," she says. "Music is also huge. If I'm working on a particularly moody brand I try to find music that matches that mood." Martinez also says that she prefers to work at night, but since she works with corporate clients, she typically has to wake up early to get her day started.

In addition to unusual hours and coffee obsessions, freelance graphic designers may also find the job difficult due to its solitary nature. Kyle T. Webster points out that while working solo can be isolating, he also teaches graphic arts in order to score some valuable face time with other human beings. In an interview on the *Business of Illustration* blog, he notes that although he teaches six classes, "these responsibilities only occupy ten hours of my week, so I have plenty of time to work on my assignments and my personal projects and other businesses." While these are typically challenges unique to freelancing, graphic designers in a studio setting may face more typical workplace issues like time crunches or problems with bosses or coworkers.

Earnings

According to the BLS, graphic designers can expect to earn around $46,900 per year, depending on their skills and expertise. According to information obtained on the job-search website Indeed in November 2016, typical graphic designers make an average of $53,000 a year. The job site Glassdoor indicated in November 2016 that the national average for graphic designers is $51,360.

Graphic designers use their art and design skills to visually inspire, inform, and persuade. They develop concepts, designs, and layouts for various applications, including advertisements, brochures, and corporate reports.

Opportunities for Advancement

Typically, the more graphic designers build up their portfolio, the more opportunities there are for advancement. Entry-level designers may start at a large design firm, taking on assignments with groups before graduating to solo work. They may also work their way up the corporate ladder to become lead designers.

Aside from building a great portfolio, graphic designers must also keep up with changing trends. As the Learn How to Become website points out:

> Graphic design is a constantly changing and develop-
> ing field. Designers must keep up with the commercial
> and artistic trends in the industry—or they may find
> themselves quickly left behind. They must also remain

current on new and updated computer graphics and design software programs, which are in a near constant state of evolution. This is particularly true for designers working as freelancers, and for those interested in advancing to higher positions within their companies.

The website also recommends that graphic designers join a design organization, such as the American Institute of Graphic Arts or the Graphic Artists Guild, in order to keep up with new technology.

What Is the Future Outlook for Graphic Designers?

The BLS predicts a reliable future for the field of graphic design, which has a projected growth rate of 1 percent through 2024. Although the BLS notes that "graphic designers are expected to face strong competition for available positions," those who do high-quality work will be successful in the market. Graphic design is relevant to all companies, particularly in terms of branding, and tenacious designers will simply have to continue to identify new brands and teach companies exactly why they need a great graphic designer in their corner.

Find Out More

American Institute of Graphic Arts (AIGA)
233 Broadway
New York, NY 10279
www.aiga.org

The AIGA features membership perks and an opportunity to connect with more than twenty-five thousand members across seventy US chapters.

Behance
www.behance.net

Featuring projects from a variety of creative professionals, this is a great site for connecting with fellow graphic designers and artists, as well as searching for jobs in the industry.

Business of Illustration
www.businessofillustration.com

A resource for aspiring illustrators, this blog focuses on what it takes to get into the field of illustration from a business perspective.

Design Matters
www.debbiemillman.com/designmatters

A podcast focused on design and creative culture, featuring interviews with designers, artists, curators, writers, musicians, and more.

Film and Video Editor

What Does a Film and Video Editor Do?

Film and video editors manipulate the moving images that people watch on television and in movie theaters or stream on their computers and smartphones. These include motion pictures, documentaries, television programs, music videos, and news and sporting events. Using specialized video editing software, film and video editors organize digital footage by arranging clips and cutting or moving scenes. They may help shape the vision for the overall project by suggesting particular filming or editing techniques or by choosing different equipment (such as lenses and lighting) for individual shots. Editors typically have several assistants (or assistant editors) to help them keep track of all of the shots for a given project.

Editors must master a variety of digital tools in order to do the work. As the Bureau of Labor Statistics (BLS) notes, "The increased use of digital filming has changed the work of a large number of editors. . . ."

At a Glance

Film and Video Editor

Minimum Educational Requirements
High school diploma

Personal Qualities
Networking skills, problem-solving skills, decision-making skills

Working Conditions
Film editing studio

Salary Range
About $48,000 to $61,750

Number of Jobs
As of 2014, about 58,900

Future Job Outlook
Growth rate of 11 percent to 14 percent through 2024

Nearly all editing work is done on a computer, and editors often are trained in a specific type of editing software." As lead assistant editor Robert Lanford notes on his blog, the two dominant editing software suites used in film and television are Avid Media Composer and Final Cut Pro. He explains, "As a rule, Avid is used on most big budget features and network TV shows, while Final Cut is the favorite . . . of indie films, documentaries, web series and other small budget productions. Take the time to learn both programs."

In addition to Avid and Final Cut, there are many different editing programs that are available for free or at a low cost to virtually anyone with a cell phone, making the work of the editor much more accessible to people looking to express themselves. As the Art Career Project website points out, "The recent proliferation of inexpensive digital editing programs, . . . along with the ubiquitous ways in which one can now show his or her work has made this once exotic, and even arcane, craft all the more accessible to all kinds of creative people in all walks of life." Of course, professional editing is much more in-depth than the work of even the most skilled amateur, but the whole magic and mystery that was once attributed to the process is increasingly becoming demystified—inspiring many more would-be editors to learn the craft.

How Do You Become a Film and Video Editor?

Education

Film and video editors typically need only a high school diploma in order to get started in the industry but can also benefit from a bachelor's degree in film or broadcasting. Film and TV production programs, like the one at the University of Southern California's School of Cinematic Arts, focus on teaching students "how to make compelling, in-demand content for screens of every size—whether it's IMAX or a hand-held device," according to the school's website. Students are taught about all of the tools of the film and video production trade, including how to use cameras, lights, and editing software. Editing courses may focus on a variety of issues that arise during filming, as well as methods for tweaking problematic footage in postproduction.

Film sound, production management, film aesthetics, and hands-on editing course work are also taught. O*NET indicates that 50 percent of film and video editors hold a bachelor's degree, 26 percent have been to college but hold no degree, and 12 percent have only a high school diploma or equivalent. Many colleges and universities throughout the United States offer film and broadcasting programs for both undergraduate and graduate study.

Internships

Internships are a good way to get experience and make connections in the industry. Although many of the big Hollywood studios offer them, competition to get these and other internships is stiff. One such internship is the American Cinema Editors (ACE) Internship Program, which is a six-week program in Los Angeles for college graduates who want to pursue a career in editing. The program only selects two or three interns each year. Those are not great odds, but Robert Lanford says that aspiring film and video editors should apply anyway. In an article on his website, Lanford says, "Everyone who applies gets invited to a three night A.C.E. Intern Lecture Series that will get you connected with a lot of other aspiring assistant editors who can turn you on to job opportunities. It is probably the best place to get started." Other internships can be found by searching film school career center websites, production company websites, and trade publications like *Variety* and the *Hollywood Reporter*.

Skills and Personality

Editing for film or TV is as much about creating art as it is about having the technical skills to do so. As the Art Career Project website points out, "The art of film editing is one that requires of the practitioner both a technical proficiency in working with computers and the eye (and certainly the ear) of an artist." Therefore, one of the most important personality traits for a film or video editor is the ability to envision and interpret stories and action through images and sound. Having an innate sense of pace and timing helps an aspiring editor focus on the story at hand and choose the best shots or scenes to create a cohesive final product. As film and video editor Thomas Griffin describes in a

GQ article, "Every frame does count. . . . A good editor can feel that rhythm, and how long that shot needs to go on for. There are 24 frames in a second. You can trim a frame or two frames off of a shot and all of a sudden it's funny. Or you can add one frame and it drags."

In addition to technical proficiency, one of the most important personality traits for a film and video editor is being able to network effectively. As Janelle Ashley Nielson of The Film Editor.com explains on her website, aspiring film and video editors often take entry-level positions in order to get a foot in the door at bigger companies. She says that when she first started out, she worked as a temp at the Fox Broadcasting Company and did her best to speak to everyone about her ambitions. Nielson explains:

> I started to put the word out to anyone that would listen that I was extremely interested in editing and eager to learn everything I could about it. I familiarized myself with all of the productions that were cutting on the lot, who the editors were, and who their assistants were. When these people would call in for parking passes, I would often ask them questions about the editing process and ask if I could come and visit them or watch them work.

Besides networking abilities, film and video editors must also be able to go with their gut instincts in order to quickly accomplish their job. As editor Alex O'Flinn notes in an IndieWire interview, "There's not a lot of time to second-guess anything, and that's the point. Go with your gut, take a risk, and if you fall down, you get back up because you have to." The ability to make decisions quickly and effectively, as well being able to let criticism roll off, are key components in becoming a great film or video editor.

On the Job

Employers

Film and video editors are typically employed by motion picture and video production companies, as well as television broadcasters.

According to the BLS, in 2014 about 48 percent were employed by film and video industries, while 8 percent were employed by TV broadcasting. Film and video production companies range from large multinational companies like NBCUniversal, Sony, Paramount Pictures, and HBO Studios to online-only distributors like Netflix and Amazon. Film and video editors may either be full-time salaried workers or freelancers. The BLS notes that in 2014, approximately three out of ten film and video editors were self-employed.

Working Conditions

Film and video editors typically work in studios as members of an editing team, alongside the project's director. Conditions may vary depending on the size of the production company, but what really sets the tone for working conditions is the project's director. Alex O'Flinn participated in the Sundance Institute Directors Lab, a month-long workshop where aspiring filmmakers partner with film professionals to shoot and edit scenes from their screenplays. In an interview with IndieWire, O'Flinn describes the work he did there:

> As an editor, I was paired with two directors, Johnny Ma and Jordana Spiro, who both came with scripts that were pretty killer. Before the Lab, I was reading the scripts over and over, watching reference films, practicing my AVID [video editing software] skills— I wanted to be prepared. When the day came to start cutting with both directors, I was really welcomed as a collaborator; as an editor, this is the thing you really hope for more than anything. When the director trusts you to help them elevate their vision, the process is addictive. It's one of the most rewarding experiences to see a scene that really works up on the big screen after hours of work.

Earnings

According to the BLS, film and video editors can expect to earn around $55,740 per year, depending on their skills and expertise. O*NET, on the other hand, suggests that the median income is $61,750.

According to information obtained on the job-search website Indeed in November 2016, film editors make an average of $48,000 a year, while video editors make an average of $51,000.

Opportunities for Advancement

Since most of the available jobs for film and video editors are located in cities known for being entertainment hubs (New York, Atlanta, and Los Angeles), an aspiring editor's best bet would be to move to one of these cities in search of a job. Of course, given the fact that only a limited number of cities are focused on this type of work, strong competition is inevitable. According to the BLS, the best way aspiring editors can improve their chances of success is to obtain experience in the field and continue to develop their editing skills by focusing on mastery of specialized editing software. Other opportunities for advancement include making a switch to a related occupation in the same field. The BLS suggests a variety of similar occupations, which include broadcast and sound engineering technicians, multimedia artists and animators, photographers, producers, directors, reporters, correspondents, and broadcast news analysts.

What Is the Future Outlook for Film and Video Editors?

The BLS and O*NET both predict a reliable future for film and video editors; the field has a projected growth rate of 11 percent to 14 percent through 2024. Particularly as more and more consumers are able to access video content online with cell phones and via high-speed Internet access at home and at work, film and video editors will continue to reach new audiences and will have more work available to them in the coming years.

Find Out More

Art of the Guillotine
www.aotg.com

A website for editors, film professionals, and aspiring editors to share information on all phases and technology used in the world of postproduction. The site also includes the *Assembly* magazine, featuring reader-submitted content.

Filmmaker
www.filmmakermagazine.com

A magazine focusing on independent films and filmmakers, produced by the Independent Filmmaker Project. Its website includes interviews with film and video editors, producers, directors, and more.

Mandy
www.mandy.com

A great site for job seekers in the film and television industry. The site includes a directory of production companies, filmmakers, production crews and equipment, as well as listings for production jobs, and castings and auditions.

Post
COP Communications
620 W. Elk Ave.
Glendale, CA 91204
www.postmagazine.com

A monthly online publication, featuring articles on all areas of editing and postproduction, from film and TV to the web.

Stage 32
www.stage32.com

Considered the entertainment industry's equivalent to Facebook, this website connects film, television, and theater industry pros from around the world. With more than five hundred thousand users, there is plenty of experience to be tapped here, along with job listings and networking opportunities.

Web Developer

Web developers create websites. They develop website themes, design the site's layout and flow, integrate graphics and audiovisual material tailored to the customer's specific needs, add payment processing if the client is an e-commerce site, set up analytical tools for tracking site statistics, and test the site's features to make sure all is working before it goes live. According to the Bureau of Labor Statistics (BLS), web developers are "responsible for the site's technical aspects, such as its performance and capacity, which are measures of a website's speed and how much traffic the site can handle. In addition, web developers may create content for the site."

Web developers may also specialize in certain areas of digital construction. Back-end developers build the framework for the entire site. Front-end developers focus on the look of the site. As The Odin Project website notes, "A front end developer will often focus heavily on understanding HTML, CSS, and Javascript since these languages live in the browser. They aren't necessarily focused on making things look 'pretty' (which is often left to a designer),

At a Glance

Web Developer

Minimum Educational Requirements
Associate's degree

Personal Qualities
Concentration, creativity, customer service skills, detail oriented

Certification and Licensing
Recommended

Working Conditions
Home or office

Salary Range
About $64,970 to $87,000

Number of Jobs
As of 2014, about 148,500

Future Job Outlook
Growth rate of 27 percent through 2024

but rather making sure that the information is presented effectively and the user's interaction with the web page is as smooth as possible." Some web developers handle all aspects of creating and maintaining a website and are known as full-stack developers. All web developers must be familiar with a variety of programming languages, including HTML, CSS, Java, JavaScript, Flash, jQuery, Microsoft Silverlight, ASP.NET, C, PHP, Python, and Ruby, to name a few.

How Do You Become a Web Developer?

Education

Web developers typically need at least a bachelor's or associate's degree in either computer science or graphic design. Computer science degrees typically split their focus between practical and theoretical courses. Practical courses usually include fundamental programming concepts as well as classes devoted to different programming languages, design and programming for the web, and development for specific types of cell phone and tablet operating systems (iPhone and Android, for instance), among others. More theoretical courses may include topics like game architecture (which focuses on video game creation), discrete structures (logical formulas and proofs), or computational linguistics (the computer science of language and speech). Graphic design degrees typically focus on teaching students how to create and critique visual communications and their overall effectiveness, with course work aimed at producing work in a studio setting. O*NET indicates that 43 percent of web developers hold a bachelor's degree, 20 percent hold an associate's degree, and 13 percent have a postsecondary certificate. Many colleges and universities offer computer science and graphic design programs for undergraduate study.

Certification and Licensing

Certification in a variety of areas is another key ingredient in becoming a top web developer. According to the website Tom's IT Pro, the best certifications for web developers include Adobe Certified Expert Web Specialist, Microsoft Technology Associate, Microsoft Certified Solutions Developer, Zend Certified PHP Engineer 7, Certified Web

Development Professional, and Google Analytics Individual Qualification. Through these certifications, aspiring web developers can learn design techniques that follow the industry's best practices and ways of improving a website's page rank with search engines. For web developers looking for more programming-heavy certifications, additional certifications include the Certified Security Software Lifecycle Professional credential, as well as credentials in Google Apps and the C and C++ programming languages. The cost of these certifications can range from free to hundreds of dollars; some of them may be eligible for reimbursement programs via the GI Bill or an individual's employer.

Internships

Internships are a good way to get experience and build a portfolio. In a *Forbes* article, web designer Haris Bacic says he earned both college credit and a modest income from his internships, which he found through Craigslist. Other sites where aspiring web developers can find internship opportunities include Indeed and Authentic Jobs. The work Bacic did in those internships helped him build his portfolio. A strong portfolio is essential. "The most crucial step is to build a stellar—not just good—portfolio website," says Bacic. "Your portfolio website should be extremely impressive. Forget about the experience required for the job. A senior web designer will look at your portfolio much more carefully than they will look at your previous work experience." Bacic goes on to enumerate some of his tips for building a portfolio even when a person does not have any clips from work experience, including redesigning logos and websites for top brands, offering free design services to local charities, and designing for imaginary brands.

Skills and Personality

Some of the most important qualities for a web developer are concentration, creativity, customer service skills, and attention to detail. In terms of concentration, since the job requires a great deal of code writing, this necessarily demands an intense focus. Being able to write complicated strings of codes for hours at a time is not an easy task, particularly for those who lack attention to detail. Thus, these two personality traits go hand in hand when it comes to building websites.

Since even the most minute of errors, such as a missing parenthesis or comma, can cause a web page to fail, these personality traits must be at the core of any good web developer. Indeed, as web developer Randle Browning notes in an article on the Skillcrush website, "Web developers like to handle big projects by taking them one step at a time and paying close attention to the details. If a web developer were building a theme park, she would love working on the details of the physics of the rides and the number of visitors the park could accommodate, and she'd work through them one small step at a time."

In addition to concentration and attention to detail, web developers must have a creative side, too. Since they design the website's appearance in addition to writing the code that enables it to run, creativity is key. Innovative and up-to-date design skills are a must, and therefore web developers must be well versed in the current trends surrounding digital media. Of course, designing any website also requires extensive knowledge of programming languages. The most commonly used languages in web development are HTML and XML, but many employers are also looking for developers who know JavaScript and SQL, as well as Flash. Learning new tools and programming languages is ultimately a lifelong process, as computer programming continues to advance. Therefore, a good developer will need to stay on top of such developments with continuing education.

Finally, web developers must also hone their communication skills in order to communicate clearly with clients. In addition to coding and designing websites, web developers must also understand the client's goal in order to design a site that will successfully meet the client's needs. Additionally, web developers frequently respond directly to user complaints, questions, and requests. As such, developers must have excellent communication skills and the ability to respond calmly to anyone who may be critiquing their work.

On the Job

Employers

Web developers are employed by all sorts of businesses. According to the BLS, in 2014 about 20 percent were employed by computer systems design and related services, while 7 percent were employed by educational services (state, local, and private), and 5 percent by publishing industries or religious, grant-making, civic, or professional organizations. Web developers are hired by a wide range of companies, whose products and services run the gamut from large multinational multimedia companies to online-only companies, as well as smaller local shops that sell to consumers in niche markets. Web developers may either be full-time salaried workers or freelancers. The BLS notes that in 2014, approximately one out of seven web developers were self-employed.

Working Conditions

Web developers typically work traditional nine-to-five hours, with occasional overtime required when working on deadlines. As the United Kingdom's National Careers Service website notes, "You'll usually work 37 to 40 hours a week, Monday to Friday. Some evening or weekend work may be needed to meet deadlines. If self-employed, you'll work the hours needed to complete the job. You'll be mainly office-based. If you work for a company you'll normally be at one site, but if you are self-employed, you might work from home or on the client's premises." However, most web developers work on-site because they need to be present to address website issues that arise during the workday.

In general, web developers say, their work environments are neither stress-free nor overly stressful. In answer to a question on the Workplace Stack Exchange website, web developer Ben Truby states that he works in a "fairly relaxed environment." On the same website, web developer JB King also notes that his work "has been quite varied over the years. Rarely have I been in a sweat shop environment. . . . In the 7 places where I've worked, only a couple had situations where I worked extra hours[,] which generally was due to a deadline." In short, web developers may experience some crunch time deadlines and work stress, but nothing particularly unusual.

Earnings

According to the BLS, web developers can expect to earn around $64,970 per year, depending on their skills and expertise. According to information obtained on the job-search website Indeed in November 2016, typical web developers make an average of $87,000 a year.

Opportunities for Advancement

Typically, the more a web developer builds up his or her portfolio, the more opportunities there are for advancement. Entry-level developers may start at a large firm, taking on assignments with groups before graduating to solo work. They may also work their way up the corporate ladder to become lead developers. Some web developers branch out into other areas of digital media such as computer and information system manager, computer systems analyst, database administrator, graphic designer, information security analyst, and software developer.

What Is the Future Outlook for Web Developers?

The BLS predicts an exploding industry for web developers, with a projected growth rate of 27 percent through 2024. The BLS suggests that demand for web developers will increase, due to the continued expansion of online shopping on both personal computers and mobile technology. Despite concerns that web developer jobs may be outsourced to countries that offer lower wages, the BLS outlook for web developers seems overwhelmingly positive: "Web developers must understand cultural nuances that allow webpages to communicate effectively with users, and domestic web developers are better equipped for this task, curtailing the work that may be moved to other countries." Ultimately, web developers with knowledge of several different programming languages and a variety of multimedia tools will have the best chance of success, adapting to changes as they come and continuing to reach the US market and beyond.

Find Out More

A List Apart
http://alistapart.com

A website aimed at people who make websites, including designers, developers, and content creators, the site features articles on both web design and development and has been around since 1997.

DZone
http://dzone.com

This website is great for sharing links to articles of interest for web developers and also offers a variety of cheat sheets, white papers, and editorial articles.

O'Reilly
2 Avenue de Lafayette
Boston, MA 02111
www.oreilly.com

O'Reilly's website includes blog posts, video content, and a community knowledge base, in addition to an optional monthly subscription to its reference books on topics of interest to web developers.

Smashing Magazine
www.smashingmagazine.com

Another site for both web designers and developers, *Smashing Magazine* includes both informative articles and lively discussion from readers concerning best practices on the web. There is also a job board and plenty of e-books to keep readers busy.

W3 Schools
www.w3schools.com

Featuring an enormous number of reference articles and tutorials, this site contains resources on virtually all programming languages and web services currently in use. Users will find content aimed at both beginners and experts, with code samples, quizzes, tutorials, and reference guides, as well as a popular forum.

Digital Marketing Strategist

What Does a Digital Marketing Strategist Do?

The job of digital marketing strategists (also known as content strategists and advertising, promotions, and marketing managers) is to increase brand visibility and user engagement with online content, products, or services. They accomplish this with techniques such as search engine optimization (SEO), which maximizes the number of visitors to a website by making sure it ranks on the first page of a Google search. Digital marketing strategists typically work closely with art directors, sales staff, and financial team members to get a broader perspective on the company's short-term and long-term goals and priorities. As the Bureau of Labor Statistics (BLS) notes, digital marketing strategists "work with department heads or staff to discuss topics such as budgets and contracts, marketing plans,

At a Glance
Digital Marketing Strategist

Minimum Educational Requirements
Bachelor's degree

Personal Qualities
Analytical skills, communication skills, creativity, decision-making skills

Working Conditions
Home or office

Salary Range
About $58,237 to $128,750

Number of Jobs
As of 2014, about 225,200

Future Job Outlook
Growth rate of 5 percent to 9 percent through 2024

and the selection of advertising media; plan promotional campaigns such as contests, coupons, or giveaways; negotiate advertising contracts [and evaluate] the look and feel of websites used in campaigns or layouts." They may also be responsible for initiating and analyzing market research, developing pricing strategies for products and services, and hiring and managing additional staff. In short, the job of digital marketing strategists is to build buzz and create consumer interest in products and services sold online. They may be responsible for a variety of accounts or projects, or they may represent either a single department or an entire organization.

How Do You Become a Digital Marketing Strategist?

Education

Digital marketing strategists typically require a bachelor's degree in business, marketing, or communications. A master's degree is strongly advised for those who wish to obtain management positions. Business majors typically learn about the basics of marketing, accounting, and organizing principles of the business world, as well as how to deal with negotiations and contracts. Courses may focus on subjects such as accounting, project management, strategic business planning, corporate finance, and business management. Students studying marketing typically learn the basics of communication in order to sell a product or service, with courses focused on identifying customer bases and different ways of reaching them, understanding how to interact with customers, and the ways in which pricing affects purchases. Courses may include topics such as the principles of marketing, management, finance, and international business; B2B (business-to-business) marketing; market research; consumer behavior; and micro- and macroeconomics. O*NET indicates that 56 percent of marketing managers hold a bachelor's degree, and 24 percent have a master's degree. Many liberal arts colleges and universities offer marketing, business, and communications programs for both undergraduate and graduate study.

Internships

Internships for aspiring digital marketing strategists are available at many top marketing agencies around the world. ReEnvision Marketing in Ottawa, Ontario, Canada, says it hires marketing strategist interns "who like fast (and we mean FAST) environments and love to hustle." The company also notes on its website that there is an opportunity for interns to receive offers of full-time employment after their internships are completed, based on their performance. A wide variety of top companies, including the mass media company Thomson Reuters, also hire digital marketing interns for summer positions. Internships at some companies are paid, while others are unpaid. All are worthwhile in terms of getting a foot in the door at a company that may ultimately offer a full-time position. Added benefits of interning include a chance to learn skills in a work setting and make lasting contacts among professionals who might be able to offer support and suggestions for future job searches.

Skills and Personality

Digital marketing strategists must have a good mix of analytical skills, communication skills, creativity, and decision-making skills in order to get the job done. In terms of analytical skills, the BLS notes that marketing managers must be able to "analyze industry trends to determine the most promising strategies for their organization." This analysis typically involves being able to effectively problem solve, identify specific goals, and map out a plan for reaching those goals, or metrics. Digital marketing strategist Lisa Gerber describes this process in an article on the Big Leap Creative website:

> First things first: We determine your business goals. Then, we get an understanding of the needs of your prospects at various stages of their decision making process. What questions are they asking at the beginning, middle and end of the sales funnel? Based on that information, we write the strategy and we outline the recommended activities to get us there.

Gerber also notes that being able to "measure, refine and repeat" is crucial to a digital marketing strategist's success, meaning that a great deal of information must constantly be assessed and reassessed in order to determine the strategy's value to the company.

In addition to having analytical skills, digital marketing strategists must be good communicators. Since they are responsible both for bringing brand visibility to the public in a coherent manner and for interfacing with many different members of the advertising, promotions, and marketing team (as well as managers and other higher-ups), it is critical that they have strong written and oral communication skills. As digital strategist Amber Horsburgh notes in an article in the *Guardian*, effective communication is important not only because it helps get the right message across to consumers but also because it prevents clients from rejecting ideas before they fully understand them. As she explains: "When clients are unfamiliar, ill-informed or unprepared they feel dumb, and when presented with an idea they will tend to reject it. Communicating your role . . . in language that people understand—devoid of a generation gap—is key to showing your value in business." Ultimately, digital marketing strategists must have great interpersonal skills, as well as great communication skills.

In addition to having excellent communication and interpersonal skills, digital marketing strategists also need to be a source of unlimited creativity. Whether advertising a totally new product or updating the branding or messaging for a classic, marketing campaigns always require both enthusiasm and creative energy to capture or renew the target audience's interest in the product. As Fresh Egg human resources manager Lucy Rennison describes her marketing coworkers, "Overall, digital marketers are a very passionate breed. Their enthusiasm for their work is contagious and I challenge you to not be tickled by some of the exciting projects and brands you could be working with at Fresh Egg." In short, creativity and passion are two of the most important elements that a successful digital marketing strategist brings to any table.

Digital marketing strategists also require decision-making skills in order to choose the best course of action for a small group, a mid-sized agency, or a very large corporation. Digital marketing strategists must make the proper decision in a timely manner in order to best suit all competing interests. While this can certainly be tricky, given the fact that many people will want to weigh in on the decision, ultimately the strategist must be able to make firm decisions with all available information and stand by his or her actions.

Finally, digital marketing strategists require technical expertise, particularly when it comes to online strategies for building a brand and web presence. Staying on top of SEO is a never-ending battle, and with new software, apps, and ever-changing algorithms for Google's page rankings, digital marketing strategists must constantly stay abreast of new developments in the field.

On the Job

Employers

Because most companies, large and small, require an online marketing strategy, digital marketing strategists can work for an astounding variety of employers. From huge multinational corporations to smaller, local businesses, digital marketing strategists are increasingly in demand. Some may choose to work directly for clients, while others may be employed at marketing agencies that specialize in digital marketing and media. A recent look at the job-search website Indeed found a variety of businesses looking for digital marketing strategists. Among these were a financial services firm, an education company, and quite a few marketing agencies. Digital marketing strategists can be employed in both the for-profit and nonprofit sectors, making this a truly versatile position.

Working Conditions

Part of the appeal of working as a digital marketing strategist is the fact that no two days are ever the same. As Ronell Smith, director of strategy for the digital marketing firm Advice Interactive Group, notes in a *Search Engine Journal* article:

> One of the best things about being a content strategist for a digital marketing firm is nothing stays the same for long. One minute you're doing client-discovery

work, the next you're working on an audience assessment or talking on the phone with a client, explaining how content, social media, and conversion-rate optimization works to inform SEO strategy. The ability to rein in chaos, making order out of disorder, is what attracts me to content strategy.

As Smith indicates, a stressful or chaotic work environment is typical, particularly before big deadlines. Digital marketing strategists may perform additional work-related duties (such as answering e-mails and updating social media accounts) outside of normal nine-to-five work hours and the office environment, sometimes leading to long days. Additionally, marketing strategists may be required to travel or telecommute to meetings with clients in various cities around the world.

Earnings

According to the BLS, which does not specifically track digital marketing strategists, marketing managers can expect to earn around $124,850 per year, depending on their skills and expertise. O*NET suggests that the median income for marketing managers is $128,750. According to information obtained on the salary website Glassdoor in November 2016, typical digital marketing strategists make an average of $58,237 a year, while information obtained from the job-search website Indeed suggests that digital marketing strategists make an average of $82,000.

Opportunities for Advancement

Typically, the more a digital marketing strategist builds up his or her portfolio, the more opportunities there are for advancement. Entry-level strategists may start at a large marketing firm, taking on assignments with groups before graduating to solo work. They may also work their way up the corporate ladder to become managers. As Rennison points out, working for a marketing agency is always an exciting pursuit. She explains in a blog post on the Fresh Egg website, "Agency life is varied and fast-paced and you never know which brand you'll get to work on next. It can be quite different to working in-house for a brand." There is strong competition in this field, particularly as online marketing continues to grow and develop, and those who are best able to change with the times will have their pick of prospects.

What Is the Future Outlook for Digital Marketing Strategists?

The BLS predicts a reliable future for digital marketing strategists, with a projected growth rate of 5 percent to 9 percent through 2024. The BLS notes that "through the Internet, advertising campaigns can reach a target audience across many platforms. This greater reach can increase the scale of the campaigns that advertising and promotions managers oversee." Thus, as the Internet's reach grows, with new social media platforms and avenues for online marketing expanding daily, digital marketing strategists will have many more opportunities for employment.

Find Out More

Content Marketing Institute
http://contentmarketinginstitute.com

This site offers some of the best advice on how content can help a brand, including industry trends and best practices, and focuses on educating marketers and marketing strategists. Be sure to check out the institute's magazine, *Chief Content Officer*.

Convince and Convert
www.convinceandconvert.com/blog

With lots of resources from digital marketing advisors, including Jay Baer, this is the perfect place to learn more about digital advertising and out-of-the-box digital marketing strategies.

Econsultancy
http://econsultancy.com/blog

With insights from across the digital marketing spectrum, Econsultancy's blog delves into specific niche industries as well as offering practical advice for branding and online marketing that applies to all types of businesses.

Marketing Land
http://marketingland.com

Featuring industry news, updates on content management systems, and new additions to social media platforms, this website is a great way to get to know the movers and shakers in the industry, as well as learn more about the world of marketing.

The Moz Blog
http://moz.com/blog

The Moz Blog is ideal for staying current on industry news related to SEO or inbound marketing initiatives.

Digital Project Manager

What Does a Digital Project Manager Do?

Digital project managers help plan, coordinate, and direct digital projects for organizations and often act as the mediators for any issues that may arise between the organization and its clients. Project managers help determine the goals of an organization and are responsible for implementing various systems to help employees meet those goals. As project manager Ashley Coolman notes in an article on the Wrike website, as the world of work continues to evolve, the job of project management has also gone digital. She explains: "Gone are the days of managing work using pen and paper, whiteboards and dry erase markers, sticky notes and the four walls of your cubicle. And saving Microsoft Word documents and spreadsheets in a folder on your computer has become a thing of the past." Indeed, digital project managers are expected to use a wide variety of online and cloud-based

At a Glance

Digital Project Manager

Minimum Educational Requirements
Some college courses

Personal Qualities
Analytical, excellent communication skills, leadership skills, decision-making skills, highly organized

Certification and Licensing
Suggested

Working Conditions
Home or office

Salary Range
About $60,419 to $84,000

Number of Jobs
As of 2014, about 348,500

Future Job Outlook
Growth rate of 15 percent through 2024

tools that allow them to coordinate the work of multiple employees who may be located all around the world.

Digital project management can be quite a complicated task, and issues can easily multiply as more and more moving parts are introduced into the equation. People who do this work learn different ways to keep projects moving forward, deal with issues that arise, and address the needs of both clients and employees. As project manager Peter Sena explains in an article on the HubSpot website, there are many different types of software that can help digital project managers in their work, including Waterfall, Scrum, Agile, Basecamp, LiquidPlanner, Pivotal Tracker, and others. Ultimately, as he points out, "projects differ in needs and complexity, but an understanding of the different ways to handle an assignment will make you a hero to the client, your team and agency leadership." With so much going on, digital project managers must be able to handle complex problems, as well as many different people all working on different parts of the same project.

While it can sometimes be confusing to have so many different people working on projects happening in the cloud, digital project management also has many advantages over older methods of managing projects. For example, Coolman notes that "work and feedback are all kept in the same place, so you can reference it as often as necessary. [There are] no arguments over 'He said/She said' or 'I didn't realize that was my responsibility,' since everything is clearly documented in one place that everyone can access." In short, digital project managers help add stability and certainty to big projects by answering questions, creating schedules and timelines, and making sure employees are all on target to meet their individual and group goals.

How Do You Become a Digital Project Manager?

Education

Digital project managers typically require a bachelor's degree in marketing or computer science. A master of business administration

Digital project managers take part in planning, coordinating, and directing a wide array of digital projects. They often use online and cloud-based tools to coordinate the work of employees or contractors who work in different locations.

degree is also common and requires an additional two years beyond undergraduate study to complete. Computer science majors typically study various ways to program computers and can specialize in areas like artificial intelligence, human-computer interaction, computer engineering, graphics, information systems, or theory. Typical classes include math courses in calculus and probability, physics courses in mechanics and electricity, engineering courses, and computer science courses in organization, systems, data structures, algorithms, and programming. Students studying marketing typically learn how to sell products and services and focus on communication skills to convey those messages. Many liberal arts colleges and universities offer marketing and computer science programs for undergraduate as well as graduate study. O*NET indicates that 48 percent of digital project managers hold a bachelor's degree, 26 percent attended some college but hold no degree, and 14 percent have a master's degree.

Certification and Licensing

Digital project managers can benefit from certification in different styles of project management, which will help them learn how to deal with both big-picture issues and smaller details. There are a wide variety of project management associations offering certification programs. According to the website CIO.com, some of the most well-known associations are the Project Management Institute, the International Project Management Association, the American Society for Advanced Project Management, the International Association of Project and Program Management, and the American Academy of Project Management. The Project Management Professional is considered the gold standard for the industry and is offered (for a fee) by the Project Management Institute. Another fee-based certification to consider is the Certified Project Manager credential, offered by the International Association of Project and Program Management.

Skills and Personality

Digital project managers must possess a wide variety of skills in order to complete their tasks successfully. One of the most important qualities for a project manager to have is leadership skills. Since the project manager is the person to which many people on a creative team will answer, a project manager must be able to lead and motivate large groups of people (or even entire departments). As Adam Edgerton, director of Project Management and Operations at the technology consulting firm Metal Toad, points out, "The best project managers know how to change the rules of the game to achieve success. They find ways to manipulate outcomes without manipulating people. They reset expectations and help the client see a better solution than what's written in the contract. They answer the questions that haven't even been asked yet."

In addition to leadership abilities, a digital project manager must also have both analytical skills and excellent communication skills. Being able to analyze problems and solve them quickly and efficiently is one of the core components of the job. The ability to explain these solutions (and how to implement them) to the team is another important part of the job, as is figuring out how best to allocate resources to achieve project goals. As project manager Ashley Johnson notes in Access Advertising's blog, maintaining a positive attitude helps project managers, or PMs, communicate well with both bosses and underlings. He explains:

> I'm by no stretch of the imagination a motivational speaker but a positive outlook plays a massive role in being a great project manager. As a PM, you are the glue that holds the project and the team together. When something goes right, it's always someone else that gets the credit and, of course, when something goes wrong, it is always your fault. The thing to remember is to always have a smile on your face.

Finally, a digital project manager must be highly organized and attentive to details. These qualities enable the project manager to keep on top of the overall project while coordinating daily or weekly tasks that ultimately will allow for the project's completion. Being able to implement systems and keep track of many different employee roles within a single company is imperative. This type of work does not appeal to everyone, but as Johnson explains, "It's the perfect role for someone who gets bored doing just one thing and loves bringing different skills and people together to solve problems!"

On the Job

Employers

Digital project managers can work for a wide variety of employers, since many different types of businesses require project management. Typically, project managers are found working for larger companies with much more detail-oriented businesses and multiple projects to keep track of, such as creative outlets like design and marketing firms. They may also work for more technologically focused industries, such as hardware and software companies, banks, international shipping, and engineering firms, among others. Digital project managers are most often found working in the for-profit sector, rather than for nonprofit agencies, simply due to the nature of the work.

Working Conditions

The typical digital project manager works in an office and spends many hours in front of a computer. He or she can also expect to attend meetings—lots of them. Meetings with members of a project team might be in person, but they are just as likely to occur via videoconference, and with team members often scattered around the world, meetings do not necessarily fit into the standard nine-to-five day. Additionally, as project deadlines approach or when problems arise, the project manager is likely to put in more than the typical eight-hour day. In 2014 the Bureau of Labor Statistics (BLS) noted that about two in five project managers worked more than forty hours per week. Digital project managers typically work full-time salaried positions, making this one of the few jobs in the digital media sphere that is rarely (if ever) a freelance position.

Earnings

According to information obtained on the salary website Glassdoor in November 2016, typical digital project managers make an average of $63,174 a year, while information obtained from the job-search website Indeed suggests that digital project managers make an average of $84,000. The website PayScale suggests the median income for project managers in the United States is $60,419.

Opportunities for Advancement

Digital project manager jobs are not usually entry-level positions. The typical project manager has several years of experience in a particular industry and also in information technology (IT). The number of years of experience required varies, depending on the organization. Generally speaking, smaller and newer companies do not require as much experience as larger, more established companies. Of course, as a project manager builds up his or her area of expertise, the more opportunities there are for advancement. Entry-level managers may start out as lower-level managers within the IT department and may advance to project management or become chief technology officers. Some related occupations suggested by the BLS include computer and information research scientists, computer hardware engineers, computer network architects, computer systems analysts, database administrators, information security analysts, network and computer systems administrators, software developers, top executives, and web developers.

What Is the Future Outlook for Digital Project Managers?

The BLS predicts a 15 percent increase in digital project manager jobs through 2024. This growth rate is considered much faster than average. This growth rate is expected because of the continued expansion of digital platforms, with scores of telecommuting workers who must work together from many different remote locations. According to the BLS, "Many companies note that it is difficult to find qualified applicants for these positions." Therefore, applicants with experience in the field, as well as a good command of the ever-changing technology involved, will have a leg up in the hiring process. Project management positions in cybersecurity, health care, and insurance are suggested to be the industries with the largest growth in jobs, according to the BLS.

Find Out More

The Digital Project Manager
www.thedigitalprojectmanager.com

A collection of digital project management inspiration, how-to guides, tips, tricks, tools, humor, and job postings, this website pokes fun at—and attempts to solve the persistent problems of—some of the stumbling blocks associated with project management in general, including difficult clients, small budgets, and crazy deadlines.

Drunken PM
http://drunkenpm.blogspot.com

A humorous take on project management, written by David Prior, this blog focuses on Scrum and Agile project management tips.

A Girl's Guide to Project Management
www.girlsguidetopm.com

Offering insight from the point of view of a female project manager, Elizabeth Harrin's blog has won multiple awards and includes some humor on the subject of project management.

Herding Cats
www.herdingcats.typepad.com

Glen Alleman provides an in-depth look at both the how and why of project management in his aptly named blog. Topics include earned value, risk, cost, program performance, integrated master plans, and integrated master schedules.

PM Student
www.pmstudent.com

Aimed specifically at students who aspire to become project managers, Margaret Meloni's blog aims to provide them with knowledge and skills that can be used on the job.

Interview with a Freelance Writer

Norm Schriever has been working as a freelance writer since 2012. He writes articles and blogs for numerous digital media companies, including *Huffington Post*, Expedia, and Hotels.com. He has also ghostwritten articles for sites like HostGator and Business.com. Before becoming a full-time freelance writer, he worked in real estate as an agent and mortgage lender and for a real estate law firm. He discussed his career with the author via e-mail.

Q: Why did you become a freelance writer?

A: I was always creative as a kid up to high school, though drawing and visual art was my focus. But I also loved reading and it was my dream to one day travel the world and explore the amazing people and cultures I encountered, documenting it all on the page. I did some periodic creative writing through college but lost that passion completely once I got into the "real world" of working and paying bills.

Fast forward fifteen years or so to my late thirties and I'd "made it," according to society, with the big house, fancy cars, and hordes of extravagant material things in my life. It was all fun, but the more time that went by, the less fun it was. The more I chased money, material things and "success," the more stressed I felt and my happiness diminished.

So I looked in the mirror one day and asked myself if this was really what I wanted to do for the rest of my life. Was this who I wanted to be?

The answer was like a gut punch, but I couldn't ignore it. So I sold or donated all of my possessions, gave up the house and the cars and the well-paying job and moved down to the beach in Costa Rica to write my first book.

Six years later, I'm still traveling and writing. Are there days that I regret it and think it was a rash and borderline-insane decision?

Hell yes—like every day! But I also truly love what I'm doing and I wouldn't change a thing. For better or worse, this is what I was meant to do with my life.

Q: Can you describe your typical workday?

A: I'm a super early riser—usually like 5 AM or even earlier. For writers, it's all about ritual, and my ritual is that I need to guzzle some hot coffee as I sit down and ease into work. I start with [the] most important thing on my plate—a book if I'm working on one—and spend a couple of hours on that before I turn to my other writing tasks of writing blogs and marketing materials for clients. By the time other people get up, get dressed, commute to work, and get settled at their desks, I'm already on my third hour of work. I try to get 80 percent of the important things I'll complete that day done before noon.

My main focus is writing blogs and doing social media marketing for small businesses. I have a lot of clients in the real estate, mortgage, and personal finance industries, since that was my field in the past. But I also work for chiropractors, fantasy sports start-ups, pet companies, health and wellness consultants, and even minor league pro sports teams.

I'll fit in a workout, a siesta, and take lots of breaks to reenergize my wavering concentration as the day goes on. Many nights, I'm still working after dinner and into the night. But it's just mostly busy work at that time, and nothing that requires too much focus.

I do this six days a week, and on my day off, I work on my own books, blogs, articles, etc.

Q: What do you like most about your job?

A: I don't have to wear pants.

Q: What do you like least about your job?

A: I don't have to wear pants, which means some days I never actually leave the house.

Q: What personal qualities do you find most valuable for this type of work?

A: You have to be self motivated to an uncanny degree. In fact, if you're not obsessed with writing and what you do, you're probably in the wrong business. I know this is for me because at this point, I can't *not* write.

Concentration is key. Self-awareness is crucial. Knowing what you're good at and where your weaknesses lie allows you to compensate. Good writing is usually always about clear, direct communication—not about flowery stanzas and fancy prose. So being authentic is a valuable quality, in itself.

It also helps to live a little. The best writers have the best stories and tell those to an audience through writing with minimal interference or interpretation.

Q: What kinds of freelance writing do you find the most fulfilling, either in terms of monetary payment or for personal reasons?

A: I treat my writing as if I was a bricklayer. There are no tricks to what I do, no shortcuts. I place each word and sentence and paragraph carefully until I've built something, maybe not pretty, but definitely something sturdy that will last. For that reason, I actually like the assignments that are slightly uninteresting or arduous. They say there are no small parts, just small actors, and I feel the same about writing—my ultimate challenge is to make the uninteresting fascinating. So I'll write anything for anyone anytime, no matter the subject matter or whether it's interesting or personal to me.

Now to really answer the question, I love writing things that I think will help people. I do a lot of personal blogging and article writing about culture, humanity, causes, and social issues in our world, and try to connect the human family through my writing.

Q: What advice do you have for students who might be interested in this career?

A: If you want to make good money, be part of a team, get appreciated and congratulated for your job and work regular hours, do something else. I like the advice that Mark Twain gave about writing: "Do it for three years, and if at that point you aren't making a living, then go chop wood."

Other Jobs in Digital Media

Art director
Brand/campaign manager
Branded content and media
strategist
Communications director
Creative content producer
Creative director
Digital asset coordinator
Digital content coordinator
Digital content specialist
Digital content writer
Digital experience specialist
Digital marketing coordinator
Digital marketing manager
Digital media and web associate
Digital media buyer
Digital media coordinator
Digital media producer
Digital media sales
Digital media specialist
Digital producer
Digital production asset
specialist

Digital reporter
Director of marketing and
digital media
E-commerce customer
acquisition
Film/video technician
Global campaigns project
manager
Instructor/professor/teacher
of digital media and
communications
Media planner
Mobile account manager
Motion graphics designer
Pay-per-click strategist
Publicist
Public relations specialist
Search engine marketing
strategist
Web and digital media analyst
Web designer

Editor's note: The US Department of Labor's Bureau of Labor Sta-tistic provides information about hundreds of occupations. The agency's *Occupational Outlook Handbook* describes what these jobs entail, the work environment, education and skill requirements, pay, future outlook, and more. The *Occupational Outlook Handbook* may be accessed online at www.bls.gov/ooh.

Index

Picture Credits

About the Author

Laura Roberts writes fiction and nonfiction for young adults and adults. She has worked as a weekly columnist, writing coach, professional book reviewer, and editor and has been freelancing since 2007. She lives in San Diego, California, with her husband, Brit.